Weed 'N' Whiskey
(Reefer, Reefer Madness & Mad Cow)

By Ray Tempus

I0807960

Weed 'N' Whiskey
(Reefer, Reefer Madness & Mad Cow)

Published By
One Temptation Press
244 Fifth Avenue, Suite D257
New York, New York 10001
onetpress@yahoo.com

www.40points.com

ISBN: 978-0-9772587-5-8 First Printing: 2008

Acknowledgements

When I decided to do the first book "A 40 Point Guide To Peeing In New York," in what has become a series of humor/satire books the plan was to do just the one book.

I thought it'd be fun to share a chuckle with others about a small inconvenience that can be a pretty serious issue if you "gotta go." How it got to book four I'm not sure. The series goes to twenty plus so by the time it's finished perhaps I'll know how I got there if it matters. Thanks to Doug and the hearty efforts of 1TPress multi-taskers; so far so good. As always the loving Father & Son, baby brother & crazy uncle in me dedicates every painting every sculpture every writing every effort to family. And it's still not blamed on you. (smile.) I'll always take this space to thank Sherry, Rodlyn, Jenna, Trowers, Don, Punkin & Anthony for everything. You've all mattered greatly. Malfi, Laura, Christine, Barbra, Shadin, Thanks for making me feel like

I matter even If I don't. Gus & Marina, Margarita, Diana Baker & Kimberly; your selfless benevolence allows me to see the light of day. Thanks. Angie, Eric, Mary & Pooja have offered such encouraging words that keep me enthusiastic about the project. Thank you.

Keisha, Makeisha & Tiffany I'd like to adopt. O.K., o.k. the grumpy old crazy guy has a heart and you all totally melt it on sight. And not because y'all cute, but because you're all so sweet and kind. I appreciate it. Special holla at Dan, Mr. Sanchez, Enrique and all the others for your participation and insight. Thank you Marisa & Claire, Julie & Jay (at the Jay Thomas Show,) John, and the crew at the Daily Sonic for shining a light on all of this. It ain't nothing if nobody knows about it. Kennedy & askanewyorker.com, Chris & Jim, Jack Spade, BCH and Ingram give us a stage. Thanks folks. Thank You Barnes & Noble, you put us " On Broadway!"
(and made us recommended reading.)

Table of Contents

- Introduction pg. 1
- Rewind
  (from Last One Gone Turn The Lights Out)
  Comparisons. pg. 5
- Authors Note pg. 12
- Commencing pg. 13
- Why Marijuana is illegal in the U S pg. 16
- Fascist Opposition pg. 32
- What They Won't Do pg. 34
  (Cops chasing weed)
- Sexy Whiskey pg. 40
- Lower the Drinking Age pg. 42

- Binge'n pg. 45
- Under Age Puffing pg. 48
- Stupid Drunk pg. 52
- Driving pg. 54
- Puke'n pg. 56
- Good Liquor pg. 58
- No Blunts pg. 60
- No Street Purchasing (Gansta Weed Sellers) pg. 62
- Somebody Wake Up Jamaica pg. 64
- Countries Where Marijuana is Legal pg. 68
- The New Public Toilet pg. 69

- 10 Reasons To Legalize Weed U.S. and Worldwide pg. 72
- Hemp Industrial History & other uses for Hemp pg. 74
- How To Grow Your Own pg. 77
- Strains pg. 82
- Hashish pg. 84
- Conversations pg. 86
- Dying pg. 90
- Ray's Middle Finger pg. 92
- Imagine That pg. 104
- In Parting (Next Up) pg. 108
- The Ray Tempus Book Series pg. 109

Well, ... here we go again.
Letters from your crazy uncle who's kept on the back porch.

Update: Thanks to my friends Donna and Patricia summer '08 was spent on a house boat.

Even better the boat is docked in New York City at the Hudson river 79th st. boat basin. B-E-A-U-T-I-F-U-L!

Thanx, see y'all next summer.

..... back to the back porch (smile.)

Introduction

Book four. But in case you just joined us this is how the story goes.... Young Wall street hot shot abandons the dough before going postal. Emerges Painter/ Sculptor. (great I might add) La di da di, All be ire. Insulted by a pee pee summons; had it tossed for L.O.E. Authored:
"A 40 Point Guide To Peeing In New York"

in smart alec response. Two more humor/satire books and now, "Weed 'N Whiskey." (Reefer, Reefer Madness & Mad Cow.)

One could get a pro-weed anti-whiskey message from these writings. However this is neither an advocation of marijuana nor a denunciation of alcohol. This is really underneath it all more about propaganda. To re-call a few years back, around September 18th or 19th, 2001 when being grilled by the press corp as to why all of the information provided to them about a recent cataclysmic event was coming from what was essentially the office of propaganda? The exasperated response of the U.S. Attorney General was, "we're closing the Office of Propaganda!" Later in a White House press briefing when asked to comment on what was said by the A.G. the Commander In Chief said, "we decided to tell the American people the truth." (pregnant pause for effect.) Decided? And who's the decider who decided this. Don't worry, we're not getting serious on you here. I'd never do that. But read on. Check out things that were said by U.S. senators to the U.S. Congress. (pg. 21-31). Read what was actually printed in main stream news papers. The ridiculous lies will surprise you in their absurdity. You won't believe anyone would believe the reefer madness propaganda.

While these things were said over a half century ago, my question is this; in the future will the things we hear from our branches of government today sound as preposterous as that crap sounds now? Scary to think the dread "T" word and, "if you smoke a joint you're likely to kill your brother," have a common DNA.

But like I said, I'm not gonna get serious on you here. So I'll stay away from things that I wonder about and stick to things I know about, like how to grow tips (pg. 77) and Twinkies.

However, since I blew my cover and let on that I actually pay attention to the real world (though I don't live in it,) allow me to welcome you to the first installment of.... Philosophers Corner. (kinda like Bullwinkles, today's poem.)

" *Though I appear to live my life in solitude I am forever in company knowing I am a member of that invisible society of truth seekers. Of which there are only a few living members on earth at any one time." —Einstein —*

Great minds? (smile)

KUM-BA YA-DUDE
DIE MOTHER F@?*!
WEED
WHISKEY
XXX

Rewind

Reefer, Reefer Madness & Mad Cow.
(From *Last One Gone Turn The Lights Out*)
Comparisons.

Marijuana Makes you lazy fool. While you are under it's influence only!! So there!
We just stated marijuana's most extreme problem. The next biggest problem is, you ate a whole pie.

- Don't smoke weed before homework or Studying for exams. You'll get stuck on Stupid.
- Don't smoke weed then go drive the car. Your perception of depth can be a little off. And those fast approaching objects can pop out of no where when slightly tripping.
- Hide the car keys & Twinkies.

Why regress to insane reefer madness days. I don't think that even the crazy neo-cons can repeat some of that madness though I wouldn't be surprised. They've already started the propaganda but the truth is marijuana does not lead to drug use.

It was a time when it was said that it transformed "Negroes," into crazed animals that play anti-white satanic voodoo music. And they were talking about Jazz. Can you imagine what would've been said if rap had been around then? The truth is somewhere in the interest of the industries that would be adversely effected by the production of industrial hemp. Not the strain of hemp with the potent flowering buds.

I'm not saying to smoke weed. But wouldn't you rather see college kids and young adults pass a joint than a bottle. Let's be honest and compare. Neither is good for homework. Period. Neither is good for driving, but booze is a million times worse.

Puff a dube, you wanna listen to the radio until you're inclined to raid the fridge. Take a sip and you want to hop in a car to go raise hell. Get a group of young people together passing the bong, they order a couple of pizza's and some ice cold coke; listen to music, laugh at nothing, denounce the government and laugh at nothing some more. O.K. so the nightclub did'nt make any money. Give the same group a couple of shots of booze; time to go "out" and have fun, Bud's driving. Though the odds have decreased, let's pray they all get back safe.

The car isn't the only thing that could be hazardous. Drunk people are obnoxious, they'll pick a fight with other drunk people or sober people. But the other obnoxious drunk people are more willing.

The land in jail factor, the land in the emergency room factor, the land in bed with who knows what factor, the puke factor. And let's face it; women's problems can be even more frightening.

I mean, college kids gather and smoke pot, then sit around and talk philosophy. College kid's gather and drink, then play dangerous games or go out and damage whatever. Just for fun. But it's back to the days of reefer madness.

To mildly poison yourself is o.k.? Alcohol is technically poison. Think about it. Drink it and

WEED
SODA
HE
HE
HE
Lazy Fool
Won't fight, ----, or run a foot race.
WHISKEY
F
SOB N
Moth@??S!
Damn Fool
Fight everybody, ----anybody, and run strait to the nearest Jail or hostpital.

your mind and body functions change dramatically. You walk crooked and the next day you're sick as a one eyed dog.
Puking on anything in our way. You've been poisoned, though be it mildly.

But I really don't have any fear per se. It's the other propaganda that concerns me. Besides you'd have to have mad cow to believe that weed will kill you.

P.S.

This is a postscript example. The actual scene took place after this chapter was written. This happened one evening while sitting in a Pub/Restaurant in midtown Manhattan. You could call it popular but there's an unmistakable Yesterday feel. Almost a nostalgic element to the place. In the early evening 6 to 9 o'clockish 30% or so of the patrons, (like myself,) are there to dine. The chef (Tulio,) is the only guy left in town to offer seconds at no charge. The bar is lively and they have half a dozen or so TV's with sports playing. The old regulars give the place a neighborhood pub feel, the other bar people make the place a real dive. This particular day as I was watching a basketball game, a commotion broke out at the end of what was not a crowded bar. One guy picks up a stool and clobbers another guy with whom he argued. He then pummels the poor fellow to the floor and beats the stuffing's out of him. The young lady tending the bar, (very pretty but a don't let the beauty fool you vibe,) rushed over to pull the guy off. Another patron stepped in and slammed the beater to the floor, although I believe cutie could've handled the deal. That guy then leaves threatening the guy he'd already beat up. The guy that got whipped was helped to his feet. He ordered another pitcher of beer.

He and the other guy had been drinking together before the beatdown. The guy who got beat up; that's the second time I've seen him get hit over the head with a large object by the person he'd been drinking with. Wanna tell me this guy shouldn't stay home and smoke a joint.

BAR
NO SMOKING
CRAZY
XXX IGNORANT OIL
ACT A FOOL
FOOLISH FOOL

Author Note:

It's worth noting here that our purpose here is not to advocate or encourage Marijuana smoking. Marijuana smoking induces heavy coughing, extremely teary eyes and worst of all snot. Your body is telling you something. It's telling you, don't take big drags in the company of the opposite sex, suave you are not.

Fact: Cannabis is <u>NOT Toxic</u>! There has never been a case of anyone dying of poisoning (overdose,) or becoming toxically ill from cannabis sativa.

Commencing
3-10-08

Sippin' coffee, puffin' a dube I look out the window on a clear day. A WBGO (jazz) program is on the radio. I sit at a table to commence writing Weed n' Whiskey. My gaze alternates between the nothing out the window, a recently started painting across the room on an easel and a news program on T.V. A particular story on the T.V. caught my attention. A young Minnesota woman died of alcohol poisoning at a bar celebrating her 21st birthday with friends.

The underlying topic was that her parents were suing the bar that served her so much alcohol and they were suing her friends that were with her and encouraging her to do it right. She was after all legal finally. I say finally because she'd already been busted for DUI twice before as a minor.

• 1400 Alcohol deaths per year for the youth, U.S. .

Is this a misplaced lawsuit? It is as it relates to her friends for certain. They're needed to make the case against the bar. But the real culprit is unsuiable, because the real culprit is the society in which we live. How are you gonna sue that? Boozing is sexily promoted, normalized and encouraged by society. Binge drinking is back.

The youth is drinking itself to death, literally. The real toll will tell years from now but the immediate toll is frightening enough. The number of ways people are destroyed by alcohol boggles the mind. Long term; alcoholism, cirrhosis etc. is the micro. The extension of effected family, inner circle of friends, etc. associated health problems, the world at large is the macro. We're focusing on the micro here.

Road kills and near kills, girl with a guy who's looking to take advantage of her, or two, or three, twelve or whatever number of guys.

Alcohol poison victims (The hang over is the mildest form.) Puking where ever and nose vomit. Fights, accidents, fool making and personal vulnerability are the micro. As well as the numerous young women who are raped and or murdered when drunk. GET REAL!! The common denominator of all the young women who were out drinking and ended up dead in recent memory is extreme drunkenness.

Booze makes simple misunderstandings not only happen, but makes this nothing something big. Unnecessary words become more. Otherwise rational people become belligerent, friction and fights occur, anything from a harmless tussle to a death match. Literally.

Why is Marijuana illegal in the U.S.?

The reason marijuana is against the law in the United States of America is because it makes white women want to have sex with black men.

(a looong pause for effect.)

Well, that was the reason given by a U.S. senator, (Harry Anslinger NY) to the U.S. Congress. Can you believe this nonsense was actually spoken in the highest branches of government? And that ain't all. But, first let's look at other possible reasons.

Maybe some rich and powerful industrialists didn't need any competition from industrial hemp. Like maybe the DuPont crew. Perhaps their patent on nylon could be much more profitable without hemp fabric (a far superior fabric) as competition. Or the Chemical Fuel industries or Timber industrialists.

William Randolph Hearst, with his newspaper empire didn't need the manufacturing of hemp paper to squelch the profits of his timber investments. He devoted countless articles and editorials to demonizing propaganda against hemp. He also used racist propaganda, but his most extreme hatred was reserved for Mexicans. He'd lost 800,000 acres of timberland to Pancho Villa.

Telling lurid lies about Mexicans and the devil Marijuana causing violence sold newspapers, making him richer. He called it the new Mexican drug and said things like, "Marijuana is a shortcut to the insane asylum. And, hashish can make a murderer who kills for the love of killing out of the mildest mannered man."

The Pharmaceutical companies were in on it, too. They could neither identify nor standardize cannabis dosages, besides, with cannabis, folks could grow their own.

This is all better explained if you Google, "Why is marijuana illegal?" You won't believe your eyes, we"ll offer a sampling, but first, check the forward to the ridiculous movie, *Reefer Madness*. When you stop laughing, read the pure bull spoken on the U.S. Senate floor. And what you see here is nothing. Look up "Anslinger's Gore Files." Some things never change.

Seems to me the government today uses the same "scare the hell out of 'em" tactics to push its lies-based evil agenda. Oh...oh, yeah the t_r_o_ _ s__are gonna _kill us all in 15 minutes if we don't send a trillion dollars to Halliburton....I mean Iraq.

P. S.
The irony here is that America's first marijuana law was enacted at Jamestown Colony, Virginia in 1619. It was a law "ordering" all farmers to grow Indian hemp seed. You could be jailed for not growing hemp in times of shortage. Hemp was legal tender, you could even pay your taxes with hemp.

Google search Reefer Madness and watch the film. You'll die laughing. Check out how the movie starts....

Reefer Madness

<u>tell your children</u>

The motion picture you are about to witness may startle you. It would not have been possible, otherwise , to sufficiently emphasize the frightful toll of the new drug menace which is destroying the youth of America in alarmingly-increasing increasing numbers. Marijuana is that drug – a violent narcotic- an unspeakable scourge-. The real Public Enemy Number One! It's first effect is sudden, violent, uncontrollable laughter; then comes dangerous hallucinations- space expands- time slows down, almost stands still … fixed ideas come next, conjuring up monstrous extravagances- followed by emotional disturbances, the total inability to direct thoughts, the loss of all power to resist physical emotions… leading finally to acts of shocking violence… ending often in incurable insanity. I picturing it's soul-destroying effects no attempt was made to equivocate. The scenes and incidents while fictionalized for purposes of this story, are based upon actual research into the results of Marijuana addiction. If their stark reality will make you <u>think</u>, will make you aware that something <u>must be done</u> to wipe out this ghastly

menace then the picture will not have failed in it's purpose...Because the dread Marijuana may be reaching forth next for your son or daughter...or yours... or <u>YOURS!</u>

Yeah, I know.
You ain't seen nothing
Yet. Keep reading.

An editorial printed in several newspapers 1934

- **Marijuana influences negroes to look at white people in the eye, step on white men's shadows and look at white women twice.**

Comment: Huh?

Anslinger—

- **Blacks, Mexicans & other foreigners were snaring white children with marijuana.**

Comment: Let us see the
data on these
missing children.

- *Dr. A.E. Fossier*- **NO medical journal 1931**

"Under the influence of hashish these fanatics madly rush at their enemies and ruthlessly massacre everyone within their grasp."

Comment: Liar Liar!

• *Anslinger-* **"There are 100,00 total marijuana smokers in the U.S. and most are Negroes, Filipinos, and entertainers. Their satanic music jazz & swing result from marijuana use. This marijuana causes white women to seek sexual relations with Negroes, entertainers and any others."**

Comment: Should he have continued with, (and once they go black they'll never come back?)

Anslinger—

- **The primary reason is it's effect on the degenerate races.**

Comment: Hey, who you
calling a degenerate you
degenerate?

Anslinger—

- **Marijuana is an addictive drug which produces in it's users insanity, criminality and death.**

Comment: Damn, they make
it sound like crack.

Anslinger—

- **Reefer makes darkies think they're as good as white men.**

Comment: Well we can't have that.

Anslinger—

• **Marijuana leads to pacifism & communist brain washing.**

Comment: Shut up stupid,
before I punch you
in the nose.

Anslinger—

- **You smoke a joint and you are likely to kill your brother.**

Comment: Especially if you drank
a fifth of whiskey
after.

Anslinger—

- **Marijuana is the most violent drug in the history of mankind.**

Comment: This stuff is so
ridiculous I'm running
out of comments.

Anslinger—

• **(His favorite was his version of the definition of assassin.) "In the year 1090 there was founded in Persia a religious and military order of the assassins, whose history is one of cruelty, barbarity and murder and for good reason the members were confirmed users of hashish or marijuana and it is from the Arabs hashashin that we have the English word assassin.**

Comment: Hey, isn't that what Bush's Secretary of State said to justify invading Iraq.

Fascist Opposition
(Why Fascist hate weed)

In the book: "Last One Gone Turn The Lights Out", fascism is defined. In case you haven't gotten that book yet: (Amazon, B & N, wherever books are sold), here's fascism defined. *If you have two cows the government takes both of your cows and shoots you. No milk, No money, No nothing.*

If you drunk the people they'll except what's been put on them, just boozily drowning in their sorrow. The Fascist don't need people toking. They'll zone out what's on T.V. and think individually, no longer excepting fascist oppression.

You see, social conditions are like banking. The banking system survives on consumer confidence and consumer confidence alone. If we the people don't have confidence that banks can secure our money and put a run on the banks the whole banking system will collapse.

If we the people don't accept the system of government the system will collapse.

Independent thinkers will not accept or be indifferent to fascist oppression. Fascist hate thinkers and thinkers hate fascist.

What they won't do.
(Cops chasing weed)

400,000 plus low level pot arrests cant happen in the short period that it has unless tons of money and manpower are dedicated to it. Put 90% of the cops on pot patrol and you put 90% of the payroll on pot patrol. No wonder rape, murder and armed robbery are on the rise, but I'll let you here it in the words of NYC's current mayor later in the book.

The theory had been that low level pot arrests were the reason for the reduction in major and violent crime. Reasoning that people who commit big crime have no regard for the petty stuff.

At first they were right. One particular incident a criminal was bagged jumping a subway turnstile instead of paying the fare which at the time was $1.25 or $1.50. This fool had not only an arsenal of weapons on his person but a huge stack of money. He could've paid a private helicopter to take him where he was going. He was also wanted for a couple of very serious crimes. There were a few other examples like this but they usually netted someone who had an arrest warrant for ignoring a court date of a petty offense like the one they'll be facing when they get to the station house.

Real criminals no longer smoke in public, they go home. They know not to get arrested with 1,000 vials of crack and $3,000 for jumping a turnstile. They pay the two dollars and get home with $2,998, 1,000 vials of crack and....oh, oh yeah the cache of hand guns, some of the rapid fire variety.

So now they're out driving up the murder rate and going home to smoke their weed. Leaving the unsuspecting construction worker at lunch time puffer, the between classes student and the hippie hearted yuppie to get caught discreetly puffin' a dube just to trip a little on their spare time. They still believe that the killers and rapist will fall into their laps by stalking joint smokers?

While these clucks are looking for joint smokers harakiri is going on right under their pot trained noses. Here is one mind boggling example that cost two people their lives on NYC time, no doubt. Three people were actually killed, but one couldn't really be avoided.

Here's what happened. One chilly night in The Greenwich Village section of NYC a stark raving lunatic stormed into a pizza parlor and shot dead the man working behind the counter. No motive, just insanity. He then charges into the street, big gun in hand. How do you fire a cannon murdering someone with the blast, then walk more than two blocks gun in hand and no cops show up in what is a business district? Where are the Cops? I'll tell you where, on weed patrol. We'll get back to the gunman.

Police departments everywhere have always said that the blue uniforms make them a target. O.K. . Problem solved, as I'd mentioned 90% of the force is wearing jeans and hoodies. They're not in police cruisers, they're in cheesy little cars with blackened windows. But they

FREIGHT DOOR

don't sit up in the cars, they lay the seats back and are reclined so that they can be hidden. They look up into some sorta high tech spy toy that's trained on a weed puffing hot spot a block away. When they spot someone lighting up they radio the foot patrol duo lurking nearby in a doorway. They sometimes even have what looks like a delivery boy pass by the smoker to be sure it's weed. The foot patrol pounces, then the van used to round up as many puffers and pissers as possible arrives, then all 15 or 20 cops assigned to the detail in this area come so that some NYU freshman can be arrested. The routine is repeated until the quota is met. (when the van is full.)

Now don't forget the gunman.

While the local boys out of blue are on weed patrol the New York City Auxiliary Police are doing general keep an eye on things patrolling. Now, they wear regular blue police uniforms. But they're not real police. First of all they're volunteers. The uniforms make them look official, but if the uniforms make policemen targets why put untrained volunteer auxiliary police in them. They don't have guns to protect themselves or anyone else. Of course they should NOT have guns! They're not police.

So the city puts a blue target on regular joe's, but put armed and trained police officers in street clothes removing the target. Now, remember the gunman with one body to his credit so far? Well two of these auxiliary boys were on the street to confront him. (with no guns.) When they did the maniac blew one of them away then chased the other one down and blew him away too. Finally a couple of our good ol' boys out of blue arrived realizing pot patrol could wait and killed the gunman.

Memo to the mayor: Scrap the auxiliary program and give us back our boys in blue. They look professional and their presence is comforting. Don't forget the cruisers and remember, Jack the Ripper and the neighborhood bandit are on to you, they pay their fare, puff weed at home and pee at Starbucks.

Sexy Whiskey

You know those liquor advertisements with good looking, smiling people drinking responsibly? It works! Booze n' is on the rise especially on the "high end." But it's all on the rise. The wine industry boast there are more winos than ever before. So whiskey makes you cool and sexy huh? O.K. .

Well, it does make many women engage in sex when they wouldn't have had if they had not gotten drunk. Every time a woman pursues a rape charge against one, two, five, ten or whatever number of men in a drunken group, (the situations have been many,) booze is the blame every time. The women's drunkenness is also the reason these drunk rapist get off.

Now it's not always this. More often a woman will have consensual sex with a friend or stranger that she would soberly never even consider.

How many young women were " loosened up," with liquor for their "first time." Before they were ready. Just hope the booze ain't the stork.

I'm speaking on women because we guys are different. We want any women be we drunk or sober. Female, of age, we're in.

Lower the Drinking Age

Have you heard about this idea? Oh Yeah, it's out there.

Not just booze barons are floating this. That would make sense. No, somebody found over 100 college Presidents to sign on to this crazy idea. No one over 20 years old should think this to be a good idea. Those heads of higher learning reason that if you lower the age to 18 it'll curb binge drinking on campus. Huh?

If being illegal won't stop it what makes them think that making it legal will? Ending prohibition didn't curb drinking.

And why 18? Why not 16, why not 12 or 10? Children that young do after all sneak into the liquor cabinet and get drunk. Why have an age limit at all. Toss the similac, pass the baby a brew. Just think, then you won't have to demonize these crazy drunken monster parents that spike the punch at teen parties. Or the I.Q. 16 H.S. Football coach who thinks it's o.k. to drunken the players at the team party.

Long Division is STRESS MAN.
SCHOOL BUS
ALGEBRA IS STRESS MAN..HIC..
BRRRRP
Guns to Glory

And what's with this age limit on tobacco products? And this PG and R rating for movies? .... NOW HEAR THIS, whiskey, smoking and X rated movies are a bad idea for children. And should the rational thinking people ever get their way and overturn those ridiculous reefer, ...I mean hemp laws (....not me of course heh, heh), at least they'll know that there should be an age limit imposed.

Like when the money you use to buy it doesn't come from your parents. Don't touch the stuff until you're old enough to buy your own. Then you can share it with me. Opps... . I mean others.

Binge'n

If boozing is up, in part due to popularizing through advertising, (sexy whiskey) young people are going to be more strongly encouraged to illegally drink.

Binge drinking is on the rise and not just on college campuses. Binge drinking is heavily encouraged in bars. It's one thing to do something as crazy as funneling in the relative safety of a college campus with classmates. (Though students have died doing this.) It's a whole different thing funneling these kids in bars in dangerous places like New York City among strangers then sending them into the street in the wee hours, stinking drunk trying to find their way home. No, they don't always make it.

Downtown bars also have a program where you can buy a booze punch card. For the remainder of the night you can have a drink at every participating bar and there are a lot of them. Oh and in case you don't know what funneling is, get this. Funneling is when the victim, I mean drinker sits up with their head back while a funnel is put in their mouth, aimed down their throat. Booze is then poured into the funnel and down the victims, yes victims throat.

Did I mention that people have died doing this?

XXX

Under Age Puffing

I say no no no. (*key the rehab music.*) Reason #1 That's somebody else's child. Reason #2, don't be giving your kids weed! Now!

Grown ups who share pot with the neighborhood youth are a complete disgrace. Yeah, they'll allow sub 20 year olds to sneak into the side door of the sparsely furnished basement that they're renting from the neighborhood widow unbeknown to her.

What this maturity challenged loser should be doing is sharing the weed with the parents of those kids. What, just because they have real jobs and own a house and a couple of cars you think they're some kind of geeks? No, they're just responsible adults that keep it from their children and their children's friends.

They also have better weed than Mr. Odd jobs. And what about sharing it with the old widow woman, she wants her reefer too.

Though her niece brings it to her she could use a puffing pal every now and then.

Been having her daily dube for 45 years, husband drank himself to death long time ago. Good thing he had insurance. He was a good man. But he's gone now so a little company would be nice.

So every now and then roll one up and go have a sit down with her. She is your landlord after all. What's more, she got the Twinkies.

Proof:

A woman in Orissa, India, who recently died at age 120, attributed her long life to good joints — the smoking kind.

Fulla Nayak said she puffed on marijuana cigars daily in the hut she shared with her 92-year-old daughter and 72-year-old grandson.

Marsha Kranes, Wire Services

think how long she would've lived if she hadn't been smoking pot. .... say this and I'll slap you silly.

Stupid Drunk

It would take all the forest's of the earth (hemp forest included) to produce enough paper to list all of the stupid things I've witnessed drunkards do. So I'm not even gonna try. Just remember two things.

1. Drunk people are sickeningly stupid.
2. It's called ignorant oil for a reason.

Closed
BAR
BURP
FART

Drinking and Driving

Noooooooooo!!!!! etc. etc. etc...

<u>Over 40,000</u> Drunk Driving Death's A Year

CASE CLOSED!

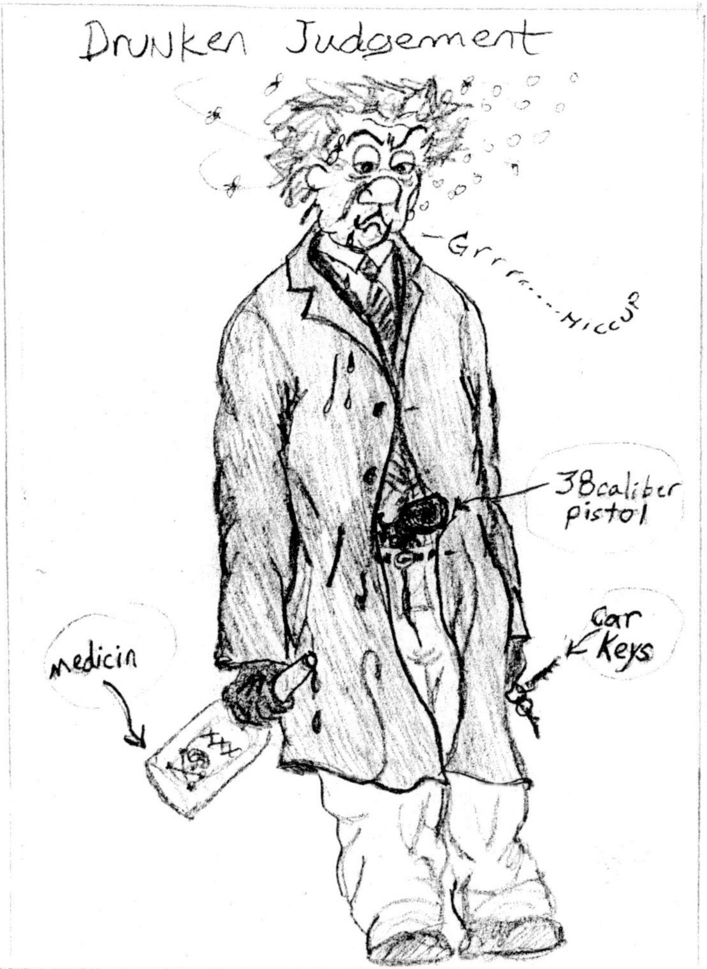
Drunken Judgement
Grrrr.....Hiccup
38caliber pistol
Car Keys
medicin

Puke n'

Puke n' is one of the worse things that happens to the human or any other creatures body. No need to describe it, you already know.

But puke n' from alcohol poison (yes the hangover is because you poisoned yourself) is worse. Hugging a toilet bowl while Hollering down to hell ain't a pretty sight. Think of what the toilet bowl is for. Your face is in a urine stained turd house. Plus, the vomit is coming out of your nose at the same time diarrhea is shootin' out cha' nasty butt. And if you happen to be spared simultaneous action, so what! You still do both.

If you're first called to the seating assignment it's just as bad. Big loud loooong stinkin' farts, flying do do and then puke. If a trash can is nearby the clean up isn't as disgusting but you still stank like swamp water and feel like death eating a cracker.

Now just think of what you look like stinkin there. Uugghh! After you throw your guts out and ruin your drawers, have a dube you nasty drunkard dog breath. It'll settle your stomach.

Good Liquor

Good liquor? An oxymoron if ever there was one.

I'm no expert on booze but I do believe there's a difference in the way wine, whiskey or whatever is made. Like with rot-gut wine, the drunkening poisonous potion is poured into the nasty liquid concoction after it's made. "Good wine" is naturally fermented and aged or whatever I guess. Many variables go into it's quality, flavor or whatever.

I imagine the same goes for beer, gin, vodka, or what have you. But, if the good stuff causes simultaneous projectile vomiting and rocket diarrhea, the bad stuff will definitely speed ones date with death.

I'll have another!
I got a whole other
foot to go!
R.I.P.
ROT GUT
RONNIE
& Good
Riddance
The
Good
WINE

No BLUNTS allowed

By now everyone knows what a blunt is. But to be sure, a blunt is a hollowed out cigar refilled with marijuana. Now lets be more specific. A blunt is a cut open and emptied cigar re-rolled with marijuana.

I've only heard of the cheapest cigars being used. Also the cheapest weed is used. I don't guess these are rules but they seem to be the norm. As a matter of fact the weed used is usually so low grade that it doesn't have any euphoric effects. It's garbage pot.

Now if you've ever made the mistake of inhaling a cigar you know that it'll make you have to lie down. Not to mention you're as sick to the stomach as a drunk. Since most of the dizzying tobacco has been discarded and only the outer leaves remain the dizzying and sickening effects are brought down to what blunt practitioners think is a reefer buzz. Garbage weed has no buzz. If you put those smelly twigs in rolling papers, a pipe or a bong nothing will happen except damage to the lungs. The cigar wrapping causes 1,000 times the damage.

Cigar smokers don't inhale and they still get every mouth, throat, esophagus, lung and whatever cancer. And please never put good quality herb in that cancer stick.

You blunt smokers should switch to better pot and bongs. Either that or just take up smoking cigars.

Street Purchase & Gansta weed sellers

Avoid this non-sense at all cost. Weed is a pacifist thing not an aggressive thing. Remember the peace and love movement, Kumbaya, the age of Aquarius? Artist and artisans, musicians and music lovers, Beatniks, Bohemians and hippies. The beauty of nature and the rhythm of life is what it's all about. Philosophy, mysticism and poetry. The riddles of the ages, and why do rivers flow. Contemplation.

You can't capture this coolness if you're patronizing some low life who thinks he's some kind of gangster with street territory and low grade pot. Looking over your shoulder and hidden hand exchanges have no place in the mellow we seek. Besides the peons that do this type of business are just afraid to encroach upon the territory of real dope peddlers.

They think it's cool to be a pusher. These losers who'll never find success at anything only help the draconian propaganda pushers to dopify marijuana. Reefer ain't dope! Got it! The punk asses even bring an element of violence. Noooo!

Think Rasta, the purpose is to get closer to Jah, to meditate, to chill. Street urchins and neo-cons are somewhat bedfellows. Strange bedfellows. Don't even speak to a person over 18 who calls him or herself a dealer and sells low grade nickel, dime or whatever bags. Hook up with a couple of horticulturally talented folks who grow it hydroponically or other wise at their house or apartment. You'll know you've met a good connection when they have a college degree, a BMW and a brain.

They'll have a love for cultivating it so they smoke it for free and make a couple of extra bucks so that they can buy paintings from their cool artist customers.

When they marry or whatever and switch the annual crop to flowers and box tomatoes they then become a pot buying customer of some cool brainiac like themselves.

Puff peacefully, think deeply and bask in individuality. Jazz is!

Somebody wake up Jamaica

Jamaica, needs to fix It's damn economy. The Jamaican government is the problem. I don't know the exacts so I wont speak on it except to say, corruption! What else could it be? Between bauxite, sugar, bananas, coffee, ganja and tourism. The economy should thrive. Allow me to make a suggestion....see Amsterdam!

The warm weather, the beautiful beaches, delicious food, beautiful people, laid back atmosphere, the rhythm, the music, the mystic,.....yes we come for all of the above. Now let's get real. It's the weed.

Tourist flock to your shores in droves expecting a spliff. You've been harassing and arresting visitors for weed and the word is getting around. People have already started going to your neighbor, (that I'll leave nameless,) because "they" understand.

How does it help your economy to cooperate with this evil mandate for the paltry

one for you
one for me

sum of 2 million additional dollars a year in U.S. aid. This mandatory passport deal is going to put a big dent in your tourist trade anyway. No weed! Why bother.

Ask your friends of the Bahamas what a super tourist trade can do for your economy. Adopt the Amsterdam model you'll increase the tourist industry by 10 billion dollars a year. Can't you see it? Not coffee bars. Rum bars, beach rum bars with weed menu's. Hottest spot in the western hemisphere.

This is traded in for 2 million bucks? Who exactly pockets this 2 million? And why is Jamaica not a tax haven? Eliminate income tax and we'll bring all of our money. The wrong people are running the place. Implement these changes, damn the queen. You can thank me later. See 'ya at sunsplash.

TREVOR'S
WEED N ICES
TREVOR'S MENU
GANJA
• 3 PRONG $
• RED BUD $
• SINSEMILLIA $
• LAMBS BREATH $
• SKUNK $
BEVERAGES
• SORREL $
• JAMAICA BLUE MOUNTAIN COFFEE $
• HIGH MOUNTAIN SUPREME COFFEE $
• RED STRIPE $
• KILLER RUM $
• TING $
EATS
• ACKEE & SALTFISH • PEPPERPOT SOUP
• EVERYTHING SERVED WITH COCONUT WATER
• CHALICE OR HASHOIL ON REQUEST

Countries where weed is legal

I wanted to offer up a smorgasbord here but doing the research I couldn't come up with any country with confirmed legal pot smoking. Many places have relaxed and look the other way policies but non stamped legal. We all know about the Amsterdam coffee shops, beaches of Ibiza and "all be ire mon" Jamaica.

But nowhere legal except an island off the coast of England called Sealand and an island off the coast of Russia called Transnistria. I don't know about you but I aint going anywhere near either one of those more than likely cold places.

But don't despair fellow summer lovers, I've an idea. We'll buy a tropical island, declare it a sovereign nation and write our own laws. Imagine that. (pg. 104)

P.S.... Update! MALAWAI!!
Just heard about it. Going to Africa!

The new public toilets are for joint smoking.
(If they ever get here.)

If you haven't yet read the first book in this 20 plus book series " A 40 Point Guide To Peeing In New York," when you get time look it up. Amazon, B & N or wherever books are sold.

It's not a where to guide it's a how to guide, because there is no "where to." Somebody, (probably some politician,) keeps threatening to bring fancy self cleaning public toilets to several locations throughout the city. Been talking about it for 20 years, they got one. (1).

You pay .25 cents and the thing gives you 15 minutes before the door opens and it cleans itself. Sounds like a perfect place for a spliff break. Instructions:

1. Have joint pre-rolled. Rolling takes up too much of your 15 minutes.

2. Have something ; perfume, cologne or whatever to spray after puffing.
3. If you gotta do-do, begin now. You need to finish before that door opens. Peeing can be done upon entering, right after puffing or just before exiting. Peeing is fast.
4. Light up. Be sure to do this in the first 2 or 3 minutes you're inside. On average it takes 6 to 8 minutes to puff a dube. You'll need time for the reefer smell to dissipate.
5. Spray as soon as the roach is out.
6. Take all of your 15 minutes and spray before exiting. When the door opens air comes in. The toilet cleans itself before allowing in the next puffer.
7. Walk away, by the time the next person goes in if any smell

lingers, they're now in a rush and your gone.

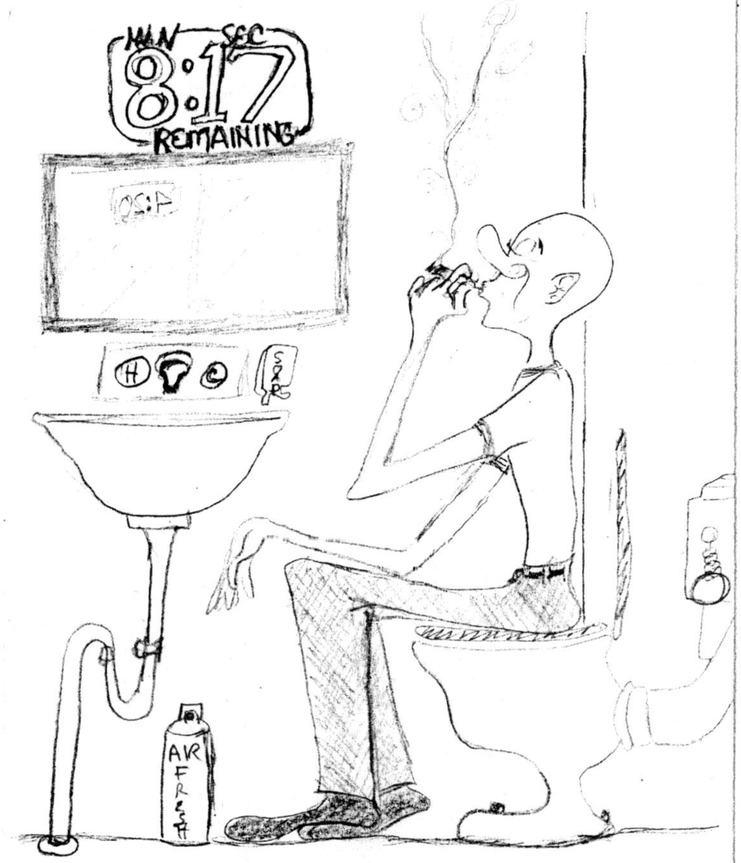

10 reasons to legalize weed : US and worldwide.

1. A new industry is born. Jobs, jobs we need more jobs. Create a new industry and you create new jobs. The bigger the industry the more jobs created.
2. Medical marijuana becomes easier to regulate and just plain easier.
3. Tens of or maybe Hundred of Thousands of criminals out of work. The mistakes they're bound to make when familiarizing themselves with a new criminal enterprise could land them in prisons where they can learn to press license plates. Tough there's no work on the outside doing such.
4. Quality control. Let's face it tokers, big businesses could do for pot what it did for booze. During prohibition, I'll bet that home brew and bath tub gin were not nearly as good as what was produced by Seagram's or whomever.

5. The price of pot will drop dramatically. Even with the extreme draconian tax that's bound to be put on it. Quality up, price down. Cool!
6. The world needs a chill pill and this is just what the doctor ordered. Everything and everybody is way too wound up.
7. So that Bill Clinton can finally inhale. (Man, he's gonna like it.)
8. It'll boost the sale of Twinkies.
9. See Industrial use. Pg. 74
10. Because I said so damn it.

Industrial Hemp
(other uses for hemp)

The three primary components of industrial hemp; seeds, fiber and hurds, have a multitude of beneficial industrial uses (historical, current and potential,) including:

Seeds — Highly nutritious foods for animals including humans. It's oil contains the highest concentration of polyunsaturated fatty acids in the plant kingdom at 80%. Omega-3, Omega-6, EFA, GLA, etc. (start your search engines.)

Chemicals: Hemp seed oil can be processed to biodiesel fuel, soaps, cosmetics, paints & varnishes, etc.

YOU LYING POLITICIANS REALLY WANT TO GO GREEN? HEMP FUEL!!
MAKE IT LEGAL. OR SHUT UP!!

The Fibers have been used for fabric since Swaddling Clothing. George Washington, Thomas Jefferson, and practically every other plantation owner farmed hemp. Rope, twine, canvas heavy ship sails, the list goes on and on. The American flag was first made from hemp. The Declaration of Independence, hemp paper. I can personally vouch for hemp fabric clothing. More comfortable than cotton or linen, but I keep having urges to set my sleeves on fire. The original jeans from Levi Strauss were made from hemp. Now that's Americana!

Paper: This is probably where hemp has no peers in terms of quality. This was the reason William Randolph Hearst propagandized against the devil weed. As I'd mentioned he was heavily invested in timberland for paper production and didn't want completion from hemp paper.

America's first economy was the agricultural economy. Hemp was second only to tobacco as a cash crop. After the age of agriculture (supported by retched doctrines like slavery,) came the industrial revolution. (The second economy) Two world class and countless other wars later.... a new economy is born. Say hello to Technology. (The third eco.. not so fast.) The industrialist who doused the growing flames of the burgeoning technology driven economy while still in the brush fire stages with their propaganda are the same ones of the reefer madness propaganda.

Wonder why America's world leader status is in jeopardy? F_ _ _ China, they're doing the industrial thing. India is building the worlds top tech economy. Hell I'm 29½ again, if I were a younger man I'd be heading for Calcutta. If they'd change the reefer laws. (laughter)

How to Grow Your Own

Choosing the best weed for growing in a particular geographic region is not difficult. The three basic Cannabis families are, Indica, Sativa And Feminized, though you can cross breed.

Sativas — Tall skinny plants. Cerebral buzz.

Indica — Short thick plants. Psychical euphoria.

Feminized — Female plants only. (No seeds, gotta clone it.) Totally euphoric experience. (Sensimilia.)

The next choice is even simpler. Indoor or Outdoor. This is decided by your own living situation.

- House with a big backyard and a high fence, outdoor.
- Apartment with a big closet, indoor.

Some plants are better indoors, some are better outdoors. Climate also matters as flowering time varies.

Many indoor growers opt for hydroponic growing. This seems to be more complex but highly effective. Now comes a million other instructions and grow tips to which I'm clueless. So pick up a copy of; High Times, Cannabis Culture or one of the other publications that we can't figure out how they ever get to publication with all those pot heads producing them. You can also goggle search, "How to grow Marijuana." There are hundreds if not thousands of websites devoted to this sport. Who says stoners get nothing done?

Personally, I've no interest in trying to grow weed but if I did I'd subscribe to the, "Brother Bell" method. It's a simple formula but first, Meet Brother Bell..........>>>>

BROTHER
BELL

Now I've observed his method several times but I don't know for sure if it works. But, here's how it goes...

On any summer day you can see Brother Bell hang n' out on his front porch chill n' with friends. Being a friend I stop and chat on a regular. Brother Bell uses a shoe box top and his AMEX card to sift the seeds away from the crushed reefer buds. He then Takes the seeds in one hand and walks slowly (Brother Bell is old,) to the edge of the porch. Next, he throws the seeds over the railing into the garden section of his yard. Last but not least, in his most authoritative and jovial voice Brother Bell commands the seeds to ....>>>>

BROTHER BELL
BE!
SOMETHIN!!!

Strains
Top 5 Best strains of Marijuana

White Widow — The White Widow reefer strain is considered perhaps the best cannabis in the world. The buds have so much THC on them that it's hard to see the green color of the bud at all. Winner of more Cannabis Cups than any other kind. On top of all Dutch coffee shop menu's.

Northern Lights — This strain has big broad leaves and large crystal covered buds and a strong hash taste. A classic plant, one of the most smoked in Holland.

Super Skunk weed — Super Skunk is a beefy original Skunk #1 strain. Matches the potency of the hashish you find in Amsterdam coffee shops. Skunky sweet smell and super tasty flavor. One of the easiest strains to grow. Gets smoked before it gets a chance to dry.

Big Bud — Big Bud was the Cannabis Cup winner in 1989 as best strain, producing massive buds with gigantic leaves and a smooth smoke. One of the worlds finest reefer strains.

Purple Haze — Purple Haze has lovely purple buds that give it a special taste and smell. A powerful strain.

Hashish

Hashish eliminates the plant matter. Several methods are used to extract the resin from the flowering buds. Processing, compressing and packaging techniques vary also. A lot of it is detailed so I'll send you back to the web or the magazine rack.

Be sure to check out the how-to's of making bubble hash. Bubble hash is supposed to be the cream de la crème.

The only method I can describe is the most natural way: If you find yourself having to handle a large quantity of high grade pot (say you get ambitious, grow some and yield a big crop,) the residue that collects on your hands needs to be removed. Rub your hands together and roll it off. Take the long dark brown rolls and ball them up together. Be thorough, this is primo. Or so I've heard.

When Nevil met Sally...
...As Anslinger turns in his grave.
(PS-24)

Conversations

I make no claims to being a Sociologist (I'm a know it all) so I thought I should speak to a few people and get their take on this subject. I decided to talk to young adults who seem to have active social lives. I asked questions such as; do you prefer weed or whiskey, percentage of your friends who choose weed or choose whiskey. I asked the weeders what was their favorite strain and so forth.

One very bright and well spoken young man offered interesting insight. He told me that he prefers weed as do most of his friends. Also that when they do drink things don't always go so well. He also explained that of the young women he knows, the preference weed or whiskey seemed to be divided along ethnic lines. Most importantly he cast his vote for Haze, as his and pals favorite strain. When speaking to a young man I've known for awhile he too cast his vote for Haze then offered that I should stop by his store soon and he'd "show" me a couple of Haze buds. (he he.)

As a matter of fact Haze was the far and away winner for favorite strain. But the most "keep it real" vote was from my man Enrique. His vote was for and I quote, "5 dollar ghetto weed." Now that's keeping it real. Now the weeders out numbered the whiskey's about 9 to 5. Which brings me to a very interesting talk with a young man named Dan. Dan always struck me as a bright and deep thinking person. When asked he replied, "I fashion myself a drinking man." He then went on to explain. Very insightful. The interesting thing was that Dan was the only one of the drinkers to elaborate. The other boozers offered a one word answer, booze.

Actually the drinkers would've out numbered the tokers but when I went to speak to a group of lovely young women they were all drunk. Their behavior, you don't want to know and I didn't want to see. But I didn't mind. (evil grin.)

O.K., but GO HOME!
WHISKEY
XXX
XXX

This.... is Haze. #1 strain

Winner of the Ray Tempus research project.

Over 100,000 alcohol related deaths a year.

According to the NHTSA there were 43,443 alcohol related traffic fatalities in 2005 in the USA. (the last year for which statistics are available.)

As a comparison, AIDS claimed 18,000 lives in 2003.

So how can alcohol be blamed for 100,000 deaths each year?

- 5% of all deaths from diseases of the circulatory system are attributed to alcohol.
- 15% of all deaths from diseases of the respiratory system are attributed to alcohol.
- 30% of all deaths from accidents caused by fire and flames are attributed to alcohol.
- 30% of all accidental drawings are attributed to alcohol.
- 30% of all suicides are attributed to alcohol.
- 40% of all deaths due to accidental falls are attributed to alcohol.

• 45% of all deaths in automobiles accidents are attributed to alcohol.
• 60% of all homicides are attributed to alcohol.

Over 100,000 alcohol related deaths a year, I rest my case.

Annual Alcohol and Drug related Death's in The United States	
• Tobacco	435,000
• Alcohol	85,000
• Toxic Agents	55,000
• Adverse Reactions to Prescription Drugs	32,000
• All Illicit Drug Use, Direct and Indirect	17,000
• Non-Steroidal Anti-Inflammatory Drugs Such As Aspirin	7,600
• Marijuana	0

Rays Middle Finger

Ok folks, time to get my rant on. You know by now that I live in the most overrated city in the universe. new york. (doesn't deserve caps). In honor of this books subject (W & W) the most overrated person in n.y. gets the dubious honor of this edition of, Rays Middle Finger.

So here's to the current Mayor, Michael R. Bloomberg who took the most overrated title from the last mayor Rudy Giuliani who hopefully is being treated for his Tourett's syndrome...you've heard him. "Hi 9/11, I'm Rudy 9/11, Guli 9/11, ani 9/11. I 9/11, ended crime 9/11, a...an...and...9/11, I'm 9/11, 9/11, 9/11 etc. etc. etc... Damn we're glad he's gone!

Unfortunately Bloomberg is worse. He's just smart enough to not let it show. So how do we loath thee, let us count the ways.

1. We loath this sawed off runt for hypocrisy. When asked if he'd tried reefer he replied, "yes I've tried it and you bet I liked it." Yet in Bloomberg's N.Y. pot arrests have multiplied by 10

N.Y. pot arrests have multiplied by 10 with 99.99 percent of them being some skinny kid puffing on an even skinnier joint on some desolate street after his psych 101 class at N.Y.U. These harmless kids are brought before an old ex-pot head judge then sent home and told his criminal record will be wiped clean if he or she doesn't commit another heinous crime for six months. Advice: Kids open the window and smoke it in your dorm room. F Bloomberg. The purpose of this propaganda. To claim to be so tough on, and successful with eliminating crime. Here's a Bloomberg press briefing on crime... "Murder is up, armed robbery is up, burglary is up, but overall crime is down 8% so I really do know everything in the world. ... and I'm god. .... So what? Public pot smoking is down, jay walking is down, elevator farting is down??? Capital crime is grouped with petty violations?

Earth to everybody, crime is on the rise in NYC!!!

2. We loath the punk for blatant child abuse in the public schools. YES CHILD ABUSE!!! In NYC's public schools children as young as 4 and 5 years old are put in handcuffs by cops if they do something really horrible like not be sleepy at nap time or crying for mommy when they get a little tired. And don't be a testy 10 year old. You'll be cuffed and taken away. Bloomberg's claim is that these monster children shouldn't be allowed to disrupt class and deprive the other monster children of learning. I believe the idea is to indoctrinate the kids to the acceptance of a police state and totalitarianism. Here's a Bloomberg press briefing on the state of education. "Reading scores are up, math scores are up, the riddles of the ages have been solved so I have singlehandedly fixed the schools so I

should be president… I'm already god." Fact: SAT scores are way down!!! The impact on education is eerily like the impact on crime.

3. We loath position buying lizard for his love of ILLEGAL IMMIGRANT LABOR which is not only a crime but a compound crime. First things first, the word is illegal! You're job is to uphold the law no matter what you think of the law. If you are a law maker and you support illegal anything you not only failed to do your job, you are a miserable criminal and don't deserve to speak on any crime. Next, because the people are illegal they are exploited in every way, the least of which being slave wage pay. Now let's get to the fact that people brought here (No! they don't jump a fence then run all the way to NYC,) are children. 12 to 16 years old. Can you say Child Labor Laws. Damn the border, bring em'. But put them in school so that

they can have a real chance at the "american dream." After all Bloomberg refers to them as the life blood of the economy, the disgraceful little slug.

4. We loath Bloomberg for his, damn safety they're only laborers approach to the extreme over building of the city. Allowing the use of broken cranes so his cronies can pocket even more money than they do hiring ILLEGAL immigrants at minimum wages as opposed to union labor at union wages. When one incompetent Bloomberg crony headed the buildings department it took a crane crashing into a building then falling to the street for this bum to be forced out. Already there had been numerous accidents; falling debris, falling workers etc, to send her packing. Enter an interim Bloomberg crony. (Also incompetent). Down goes another crane. No joke. Turns out

the crane had replacement parts that were scavenged from other broken cranes. Now hear this Everybody's negligent. Bloomberg and his cronies neither of which had the proper credentials for the job. You'd think Bloomberg would hire someone with the proper credentials and experience no matter how far & wide you must search to find them. The requirements are the person must be a licensed architect as well as an engineer. Since Bloomberg has no such cronies what he proposes is a change. He believes the head of the department should need no professional qualifications what so ever. All they should need in his book is to kiss his butt and have a bus pass. He believes the person under them needs to be qualified. Why not just put your incompetent friends under the qualified person? Or better yet just pay your cronies to hold the construction flag. They might be able to actually do that. Maybe. Oh and about Child abuse, I mean education. Bloomberg believes kindergarteners should have standardized test. Yeah right, get a room full of 5 yr olds to sit and concentrate on a 90 minute, 60 minute, 20 minute or whatever minute exam is a down right cruel thought. Anyone can tell you that's a horrid idea. Maybe somebody aught a give this guy a history lesson on Kindergarten. It's derived from children's garden. Start there and then move the guy forward. Oh... oh yeah, we're talking about god here. Crazy me. That's number five/5.

5. We can't loath enough when it comes to bad things for children.
6. We loath Bloomberg for the severe decline in expected behavior of the local police force. First he takes most of the police cruisers off of the street and replaces them with cheesy

looking undercover cars with blackened windows that don't fool anybody. Then away with the spiffy blue uniforms. Baggy jeans and hoodies are the dress of Bloomberg's cops. But they may as well dress like thugs they act like thugs which isn't exactly new but there used to be the appearance of oversight. On two occasions one a shooting, (leaving a person dead), and the other a pistol whipping beat down, the cops involved didn't even bother to try the regular blue wall of silence cover up. They just went home. This is just the beginning of what happens when you suspend professional appearance and expected behavior and send out a roving pack of thugs that look and act like stalkers. So if their misdeeds don't make front page news zero oversight happens even when strongly recommended by the civilian complaint review board. There's always been a large rogue element in the police department. Now the NYPD is just plain ol' thuged Out.

7. We loath Bloomberg for his constant buying of people to get them to see things his way.
8. We loath Bloomberg for being a sneaky little liar.
9. We loath Bloomberg for being a phony.
10. We loath Bloomberg for being ugly.
11. We loath Bloomberg because he talks like a girl.
12. We loath Bloomberg because it's common knowledge that at his company Bloomberg LLC women are mistreated and demoted for infractions like getting pregnant. His own suggestion to one such woman was to "Kill it." (She should've pimp slapped his short punk-ass) We could go on and on but we'd have to keep thinking about the worm. Used to be if you asked people about him he was widely liked. Myself included. But ask

around these days. You think I'm rough. I've never seen such a drastic swing across the board with general perception of anybody. Even gone is the admiration for being so enormously successful with the juggernaut of a company that he founded and guided to be probably the number one company of it's type in the country. Look closer. A fledgling little company gets a 30 million dollar account from what was then the worlds largest Investment banking firm? Ya gotta be connected. Cold calling or door knocking ain't netting 30 million in one shot. I'm not suggesting anything I'm just saying that with a 30 million start I'd like to think I may be able to do o.k. . He did guide it to be a multi billion dollar company so the little fellow is brilliant and a whole lotta other cool stuff. We acknowledge anyone's accomplishments. Even if they make us puke. But if he's such a leader and visionary why does he <u>follow</u> the Manhattan Institute's evil agenda just like his predecessor. So here's to you Michael R. Bloomberg, you puny lizard. You've earned Ray's middle finger. Take it and take your temperature with it. Zero(0°) Fahrenheit.

Again, annoy the crazy guy and you too will get Ray's Middle Finger.

LORD BLOOMBERG
Petty crime is way down
Illegal immigrants are the life blood of our failing economy,
I, I, I, I, I, ect
at least my pals are still making a killing
Power taste sooo... sweet!
I'm GOD.
For his people
For the people
MANHATTAN INSTITUTE
BROKEN CRANE Company

Imagine That

Welcome to the first installment of: Imagine That.

Here we foolishly dream of good things. A better world, a better place in the world. A Utopia .

Our first imagining will be, "Utopiland," A place that old hippies can live in peace; or die in peace. A place for true Bohemians to chill and other really cool spirits can at least vacation. (What, like we don't need an economy too.) No cash, bring the few things we'll need. We have what you need. First let's define Bohemian. Bohemian: Followers of art, literature, music or similar pursuits with an individualistic approach to life that's unaffected by opinions of others.

So calling all beatniks & bohemians, true rasta's & hippies, life lovers and cute women...O.K. I digressed. I'm a guy. Besides, great painters need models. But you feel me right.

Let's all be vegan and be-friend our bovine. We'll feed them grass not sheep, we won't give them Anslinger Mad Cow like that Hearst guy had. They'll meander freely offering a friendly, "mooo mon"as people pass. Just think; no liars, no industrialist, no capitalist, no fascist, no criminals, no phonies, no programmed people, no T.V., no democrats or republicans, no drunks or druggies, no racist or race, no greed, no V.D. (yes you'll be tested,) no religious denominations, no government or any other assaults on our sensibilities. Just free reign for happiness. Warm weather, quiet beaches, wine, weed & song. Food and water provided by mother nature. True Hedonism.

Notice: stressed out, tattoo 'd self loathing, blame it on society malcontents with multiple piercings need NOT apply. We don't like you either. And sit up straight.

Keep the faith cool people, we'll find it. See 'ya in Utopiland. Imagine that.

Hedonism: he- do -nism- the pursuit of pleasure.

In Parting

So...Before we descend further into the social abyss, STOP! Put down that ignorant oil and turn off that idiot box.

Oh and about the Mad Cow.....Yeah, you gotta have Mad Cow to believe a word "They" say. And you know who "They" are.

Next Up : Phoney as a $3 dollar bill.

The Ray Tempus Book Series

- A 40 Point Guide To Peeing In New York

* Last One Gone Turn The Lights Out

- Table Manners or the Lack of Table Manners

- Weed 'N' Whiskey

Next

- Phony As A Three Dollar Bill

www.40points.com

Booze batters brains

Booze waters down your mind and leads to long-term loss of brain volume, according to a disturbing new study.

Researchers had wanted to see if moderate alcohol consumption — proven to be heart-healthy — could help save the brain.

"My expectation [was] that it would [be protective], and it didn't turn out that way," said Wellesley College researcher Carol Ann Paul, who collected data while employed at Boston University.

Paul bluntly wrote in the Archives of Neurology that booze and brain loss go hand-in-hand.

"In contrast to studies on cardiovascular disease, this study found that moderate alcohol consumption was not protective," Paul wrote. "Rather, the more alcohol consumed, the smaller the total brain."

The study focused on 1,839 Americans between 33 and 88, who reported their drinking and submitted to brain MRIs between 1999 and 2001.

Heavy drinkers — those who downed at least 14 drinks per week — had a brain that was an average of 1 percent smaller compared to teetotalers.

with Post Wire Services

NOW!

THE END ☺